Disaster in the Indian Ocean
Tsunami 2004

A woman waits with her daughter to be air-lifted out of Aceh, ten days after the tsunami killed her husband and her other children.

Mitchell Lane
PUBLISHERS

P.O. Box 196
Hockessin, Delaware 19707

Titles in the Series

MONUMENTAL MILESTONES
GREAT EVENTS OF MODERN TIMES

Disaster in the Indian Ocean
Tsunami 2004

A woman waits with her daughter to be air-lifted out of Aceh, ten days after the tsunami killed her husband and her other children.

John A. Torres

Printing   3   4   5   6   7   8   9
    Library of Congress Cataloging-in-Publication Data
Torres, John Albert.
    Disaster in the Indian Ocean, tsunami 2004 / by John A. Torres.
        p. cm. — (Monumental milestones)
    Includes bibliographical references and index.
    ISBN 1-58415-344-X (lib. bd.)
    1. Indian Ocean Tsunami, 2004—Juvenile literature. 2. Tsunamis—Indian Ocean—Juvenile literature. 3. Search and rescue operations—Indian Ocean—Juvenile literature. I. Title. II. Series.
GC221.5.T665 2005
909'.09824083—dc22
                                                        2005004245

ISBN-10: 1-58415-344-X   ISBN-13: 978-1-58415-344-3

ABOUT THE AUTHOR: John A. Torres is an award-winning journalist covering social issues for *Florida Today Newspaper*. John has also written more than 25 books for various publishers on a variety of topics. He wrote *P. Diddy*, *Clay Aiken*, *Mia Hamm*, and *Fitness Stars of Bodybuilding* for Mitchell Lane Publishers. In his spare time John likes playing sports, going to theme parks, and fishing with his children, step-children, and wife, Jennifer.

PHOTO CREDITS: Cover, pp. 1, 3—John A. Torres; p. 6—AFP/Getty Images; p. 8—Frans Dellian, Stringer/Associated Press; p. 12—AFP/Getty Images; pp. 14, 17, 19, 20, 22, 25, 30, 35, 40, 47—John A. Torres; p. 28—Andrea Pickens. p. 36—David Longstreath/Associated Press.

AUTHOR'S NOTE: See p. 47.

PUBLISHER'S NOTE: This story is based on the author's extensive research, including his personal trip to Indonesia in January 2005 where he witnessed the devastation first-hand and spoke to dozens of survivors for this book.

The internet sites referenced herein were active as of the publication date. Due to the fleeting nature of some web sites, we cannot guarantee they will all be active when you are reading this book.

MONUMENTAL MILESTONES
GREAT EVENTS OF MODERN TIMES

Contents

Disaster in the Indian Ocean Tsunami 2004

John A. Torres

*For Your Information

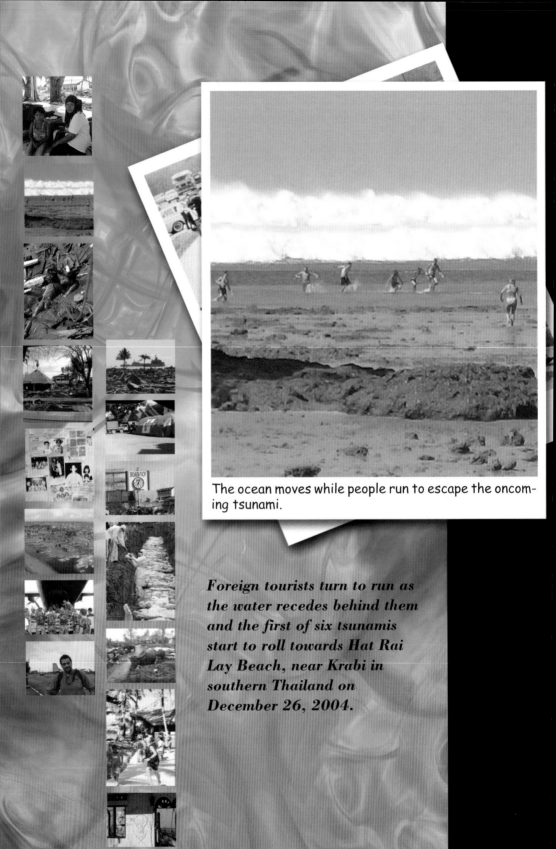

The ocean moves while people run to escape the oncoming tsunami.

Foreign tourists turn to run as the water recedes behind them and the first of six tsunamis start to roll towards Hat Rai Lay Beach, near Krabi in southern Thailand on December 26, 2004.

The Ocean Moved

It was the day after Christmas and ten-year-old Tilly Smith was having the vacation of her young life.

She was far away from her cold and snowy England home. Instead, Tilly was playing on one of the world's most beautiful beaches. Her family had decided to spend the holidays soaking up the sun in Phuket (POO-KET), Thailand (TIE-land). This morning she was showing her seven-year-old sister how to build sand castles.

The water was cool and refreshing and the sun was hot. Tilly's mom and dad lay in nearby beach chairs enjoying the morning air.

It was a perfect day.

After a while, Tilly started noticing a few things that made her think. The first weird thing was that lots of little crabs started to leave the water and head up onto the sand. Nobody but Tilly seemed to notice. A few seconds later, the ocean water was heading out toward the ocean. Water always goes back after every wave, she thought, but never as much as this. This was definitely weird.

Tilly stood up and looked out at the running crabs and the faraway ocean water. She looked around. Nobody else on the beach seemed to notice what was going on.

She plopped herself back down on the sand and continued playing with her sister. But something just did not feel right. Tilly stood back up and saw that the water out at sea was turning white. It appeared to be boiling or bubbling. Then she noticed that the boats and ships out at sea

were bobbing up and down like toys in a bathtub. Other people on the beach were noticing now too.

Then the girl remembered a school lesson she had learned just before Christmas from Mr. Kearney, her teacher in England. She ran to her mother and explained that all of the warning signs were there and that everyone had to run from the beach right away. There was a tsunami coming!

"I recognized what was happening and had a feeling there was going to be a tsunami," she would later say. "I told Mommy."[1]

Tilly's parents looked up and saw that the ocean was indeed acting funny. They believed their little girl and yelled to everyone to leave the beach. The family ran into the beachside hotel and told workers. The hotel was evacuated as people ran from their rooms. Seconds later, ocean water crashed over the beach and into the hotel itself, destroying everything in its path.

Tilly was a hero; she saved hundreds of lives by recognizing the warning signs of a tsunami.

Unfortunately, stories like Tilly's are rare. The tsunami that struck Southeast Asia the morning of December 26, 2004, would kill more than 212,000 people.

It will be remembered forever as the worst natural disaster of our lifetimes, and maybe of all time.

~

In the city of Banda Aceh (bon-da AH-CHAY), Indonesia (in-doh-NEE-zheh), people started panicking early in the morning when they felt a powerful earthquake. It measured 9.0 on the Richter scale.

Wong Li Khiun started praying when she felt the earth move. Along with her husband and her three-year-old son, she took cover. After the earthquake stopped, she started cleaning the mess. Many objects that had been hanging on walls or displayed on shelves had fallen to the floor. The house was a mess, but at least her family was safe.

Two people got swept away and perished by the tsunami that hit Banda, Aceh, on December 26, 2004. This is one of the worst tsunamis ever recorded in history.

An Acehnese man (right), ties a rope to a woman trying to rescue her.

There was a knock on the door. It was still very early in the morning, so Wong Li was startled. Soldiers were just outside. Her heart began to beat very fast.

"Hurry," they said. "You must leave now. The water is coming."

Wong Li stepped outside. All of her neighbors were running down the street, away from the ocean. She climbed onto her husband's motorcycle, clutching him and their baby. They started driving, but the water came upon them very quickly. The motorcycle's engine got wet and stalled. They got off the bike and started running.

Wong Li's husband wasn't sure if his mother and father had evacuated. He had to go back and check. He wouldn't be able to live with himself if he didn't check on them. He told Wong Li to keep running. He would soon catch up. She did not want to go without him but had little choice.

By then the water was rising even faster and was littered with debris. Even though she was now a mile from the ocean, the water had risen to her hips, and it was getting deeper by the second. Then a great surge of water rushed past them, and she and her son were swept into the raging tide.

Wong Li grabbed on to a utility pole. She clutched it tightly with one arm and held on to her precious son with the other. Within seconds, dozens of other people had the same idea. The water was roaring past her. She did all she could to hold on. There was no more room for people to hold on to the pole, yet many more came. If people didn't grab the pole, they would get swept away and surely drown.

Wong Li could not maintain her grip. There were too many people. She was being pushed off. She closed her eyes and tried to hold on with all her might, but she could not. Her fingers slipped off the utility pole, and her son slipped off her.

She and her son were swept away by the roaring waters.

"I could see my son trying to swim, but he couldn't," she cried later at a refugee camp in the city of Medan (may-DAHN) on Sumatra (soo-MAH-trah). "He kept going under the water and I could hear him yelling, 'Mommy, Mommy!' Then he was gone."[2]

A few hours later, when the water finally receded, Wong Li found her husband. She could not look up at him, and she could not stop crying.

"Where's the baby?" he asked her, tears now streaming down his face.

"He's gone," she said.

They later found the bodies of his parents and their son in the same area. Theirs were among hundreds of other bodies of people who had been drowned by the killer tsunami. Wong Li's house was destroyed and her life was ruined. She moved to a refugee camp with hundreds of other survivors who lost their homes. Her life will never be the same.

~

In Port Blair, India, a thirty-year-old police officer named Sanjeev Kumar was credited with saving 600 people, helping them escape the monstrous waves. But Kumar could not save himself.

Stationed on the small island of Katchall (CAT-chul), Kumar was one of the first people to see the giant waves forming at sea. He called police headquarters to alert them to what he had seen. He called his wife and told her to take their one-year-old son and go to higher ground.

Then this brave policeman raced along the shoreline, screaming to villagers and fishermen to get away from the beach. He told them to race up the hill to the temple compound. People huddled together there as wave after wave came crashing down onto the small island.

While making trip after trip from the temple to the beach, Kumar saw four children who had lost their parents. He ran toward them and scooped them up, holding two children under each arm. He carried them up the big hill to safety. When he made it up to the temple compound, an old woman asked him if he could get something very valuable to her that she had left behind in her home.

On his way down to her house, Kumar was swept away by an enormous wave. He died instantly.

"I screamed behind him, asking him not to go," said his wife, Deepika Kumar. "He just waved his hand and told me to go back to the temple."[3]

Never before had there been a tsunami like this. The waves spread from the southeastern part of Asia all the way to the east coast of Africa. By the end of the day, the undersea earthquake and killer tsunami had caused damage and taken lives in the following eleven countries: Indonesia, Sri Lanka (sree LAHNG-kah), India, Thailand, Malaysia (muh-LAY-zheh), Myanmar (MYAN-MAR), Bangladesh (bahn-gleh-DESH), Maldives (mall-DEEVS), Somalia (so-MAH-lee-ah), Kenya, and Seychelles (say-SHELL).

The disturbance in the ocean was so strong, in fact, that a ripple effect was felt a day later all the way in Cape Canaveral, Florida, where a sea level was recorded 13 inches above normal. Similar water-level changes were observed farther north, in New Jersey, as well.

Some countries, including the United States, have warning systems set up to let people know if a tsunami or tidal wave is coming. It would give people time to evacuate if they had to. But poor Asian countries such as Indonesia, Sri Lanka, Thailand, and India did not have such a system.

The first reports of the tsunami claimed that 8,000 people had died. Over the next few hours and days, that number would top 200,000, as more and more missing people were found dead—or were never found at all.

This wasn't a tragedy for just Asia. This was a tragedy for the world.

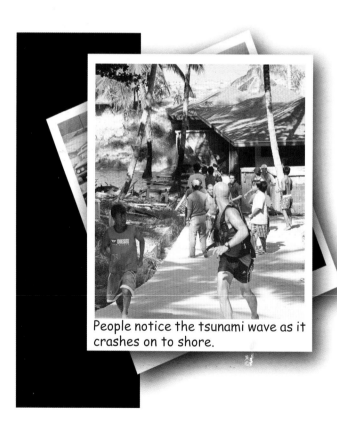

People notice the tsunami wave as it crashes on to shore.

Some people start to run from the tsunami while others stand in awe and disbelief. It was said that the photograher of this photo caught a picture of this first wave and then retreated to higher ground, watching while several more waves crashed ashore destroying the buildings that appear here.

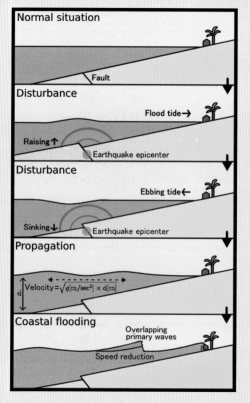

Tsunami is a Japanese word that means "harbor wave." Tsunamis are caused mainly by undersea earthquakes or volcanic eruptions, but they can also be caused by landslides or a big meteor landing in the ocean. The 2004 tsunami was caused by an earthquake 100 miles off the western coast of the Indonesian island of Sumatra. The earthquake occurred 6.2 miles below the surface of the ocean. Two huge tectonic plates under the sea crashed together. One plate pushed the other plate up, causing the seafloor to lift and pushing up the ocean above it. The ocean formed one giant wave that split into two waves. The first wave moved out into the ocean toward Africa, while the other wave moved toward Sumatra's shore.

Unlike tidal waves, tsunami waves are not very tall, but they are very long and very fast. A tsunami can be more than 100 miles long and reach speeds of 500 miles per hour. The currents under one of these waves travel in a huge circle and carry a tremendous amount of energy. When the wave nears the shore, the bottom of the wave slows down and pulls water out from the shore. Water at the top of the wave continues to build. Walls of water called bores form. They can reach heights of fifty feet or more. If strong enough, these bores will destroy anything in their path. In Meulaboh (MOO-la-bow), Indonesia, the bores destroyed even strongly built concrete homes throughout the city.

Water rushing out to sea and a large wave building on the horizon are some of the signs that Tilly recognized when she warned her parents that a tsunami was coming.

A woman surveys the damage left behi
tsunami in Sumatra, Indonesia.

Some of the early estimates predicted that 80 percent of Meulaboh's population was killed by the killer waves. The devastation of this natural disaster will live on forever in the lives of the people who survived it.

Aftermath

On December 27, two days after Christmas, the Western world woke to the news of the tsunami. Even though early reports estimated 8,000 dead, those who knew the region had a bad feeling. They knew the number would go much higher.

Most of the areas affected by the killer waves were in poverty-stricken areas. Most of the people there would have been living in poorly built houses. Generally, their governments lacked the funds to build emergency warning systems. They also lacked sufficient plans for dealing with natural disasters.

Dr. Muzzafar Sheikh, a leader of Florida's Muslim community and a native of India, said the first thing he did was to pray. He knew that many more people would be reported dead in the days to come.

"After I prayed, I was glued to the television," he said. "I could not sleep."[1]

Indeed it was a day or two after the tsunami that the pure horror of what had occurred began to sink in. Mothers across the region were searching for babies who would never come home. Brothers searched for sisters, daughters searched for fathers. Houses were reduced to rubble and splintered wood. Entire villages were flattened or swept away. Cars were upside down and rendered useless. Boats had washed up miles and miles inland from the ocean or nearest beach. The tsunami had formed new canals and brackish streams through people's houses and backyards. Everything, absolutely everything, was covered in mud.

And dead bodies were everywhere.

As the ocean water began to recede and go back to its normal majestic self, the tides continued to return thousands of dead to the beaches. Bodies were found stuck in mud. Others were seen floating by in rivers.

With the increased carnage, the true scope of suffering began. People started to realize that their loved ones were dead and their lives would be changed forever.

Zuli Nuzuli of Banda Aceh, Indonesia, always considered himself to be a lucky man. Blessed with good health and a large family, Nuzuli also had the kind of job that many people dreamed about. He worked for the Indonesian Olympic Committee. His job was to search the country for talented athletes who could represent Indonesia in the Olympic Games. He loved sports. His two favorites were boxing and running.

A former athlete himself, Nuzuli ran for his life the morning of December 26.

"When I heard the tsunami was coming, I took my family members and we ran to higher ground," he said. "We ran toward the airport where we thought it would be safe."[2]

Nuzuli and his family stayed there for about an hour before thinking it was safe enough to go and check on their house. They headed home.

"But then we saw more and more people running to the higher ground to escape the water," he said. "We knew more waves were coming."

Four hours later, Nuzuli went back to his house, which suffered only a little water damage. Again, he considered himself lucky.

Then he realized something. His oldest daughter, the eighteen-year-old, had not been home when the tsunami struck. He spent the next few weeks looking for her, though he accepted that she had been taken by the tsunami and would be gone forever.

"I know I am still lucky," he said, smiling through the blur of tears streaming down his face. "I will keep looking for her, but I know that many people lost more than I did. I still have my other children."[3]

In the country of Sri Lanka, where 12,000 children went missing from the coastline, mothers and fathers spent days combing the beach, looking for some sort of clue that their children were still alive.

Pictures of missing children and families dominate the bulletin boards of a refugee camp in the city of Medan in Sumatra, Indonesia. Many people hovered around the bulletin boards to see if they recognized any of the missing people.

These are some of the pictures of missing children and families.

Religious beliefs in Sri Lanka, which are mainly Hindu and Buddhist, make it hard for people to believe in death without a body. Thousands of parents, therefore, would not admit that their children had perished. Some said that they were looking for the ghosts of their children on the beach.

Both Hindus and Buddhists also believe in temperamental gods, ones who would punish bad people by sending a killer tsunami. This belief left hundreds of thousands of people blaming themselves for what happened.

"Hindus use the deities to think about and explain happenings like the tsunami as destructive acts of a god," said Richard Davis, a professor at Bard College in New York.[4]

Religious beliefs also played a part in how the dead bodies were handled. While the affected Hindu nations could cremate the bodies that were piling up faster than they could be buried, Muslims prohibit cremation. In places like Indonesia, volunteers spent weeks looking for and then digging graves for dead bodies. Having the bodies exposed for so long in the heat brought up the real danger of diseases forming.

In some areas, mass graves were dug. Sometimes officials photographed or otherwise recorded who was being buried. Survivors would be able to find out if loved ones had perished. Other times, no records were kept. Bodies were simply dumped in a grave and covered, remaining anonymous.

Besides the spiritual struggles—grieving for lost loved ones and feelings of guilt or that a god had abandoned them—the tsunami's aftermath also brought many physical struggles for the survivors. There were now hundreds of thousands, possibly millions, of people whose homes had been destroyed, who suddenly found themselves without jobs, without food to eat or water to drink.

Immediately after the tsunami, many of the world's nations promised financial help. Some, like the United States, Australia, and Singapore, offered to send troops to help as well. But the situation was so dire, the disaster was so immense, where would people start? What was the most pressing thing to do?

Adding to the difficulty of distributing aid was the fact that many of the main roads had been wiped out. Mark Carlson of the U.S. Embassy in Jakarta (juh-KAR-tuh), Indonesia, said one of the first things they did was to fly over remote areas in helicopters to assess the situation.

"We flew over some of the areas in northern Sumatra," he said, shaking his head in disbelief. "You wouldn't believe what that area looked like."

He continued, "There were some areas, some villages existed that weren't even on maps. People were lighting fires and waving flags so that we could see them and help them."[5]

Soldiers from the affected countries were sent to the scenes of the worst destruction. Goal number one: Find the survivors.

Although so many thousands had perished, in the days and weeks that followed, there were some amazing survival stories.

The Royal Singaporean Air Force provided helicopter lifts in and out of Aceh, Indonesia. From above, the tsunami's destruction is evident. Rubble has replaced homes along the Indian Ocean shore line.

A view of the destructive tsunami from a helicoper.

Seventy-year-old Muhammad Zaini was found by rescuers eleven days after the tsunami. He had gotten trapped under the rubble of his house when it crashed down around him.

"I no longer remember how I survived," he said. "I only drank the water that lay around me, and I could not move my body."[6]

Soldiers and rescue workers transported Zaini to a military hospital, where he was expected to survive. The miracle was tainted by tragedy, however. His wife and all six of his sons had died in the disaster.

Reporters and rescue workers wanted to know how Zaini survived. He said it must have been a miracle. Perhaps some divine intervention had been involved. Zaini claims to remember being fed by birds while he waited for rescuers.

Another man, off the coast of India, stayed alive on his fishing boat for thirteen days until he was discovered by people on another boat.

There was even an infant, twenty days old, who was found alive, floating on a mattress. She was reunited with her mother.

Despite these miraculous tales, they were far too few. Most of the people who got caught up in the swirling currents of the tsunami drowned. Shortly after rescue efforts started, local governments, from Thailand to Indonesia, realized that the massive efforts were too big for them to handle alone. They would need help, and lots of it. For some countries, the decision to accept help—especially from foreign soldiers—was not an easy one.

"Remember," said Chris Cole, a Baptist missionary working in Jakarta, "Indonesia has never had foreign troops on its soil since they gained independence [in 1949]. To them this is a very big thing."[7]

Indeed, the chain of islands in Southeast Asia, known as Indonesia, would soon have to open its doors to soldiers from all over the world.

Light, nutritious food, such as these cases of ramen noodles, are perfect items to be airlifted to devastated areas, because they do not weigh much and are inexpensive.

Here, soldiers load a French cargo plane with food and supplies.

At the time of the 2004 tsunami, the U.S. military was involved in a war against terrorism. There were active campaigns taking place in Afghanistan as well as in Iraq. The United States was fighting Islamic extremists, who had been behind terrorist acts on U.S. soil. On September 11, 2001, terrorists had hijacked U.S. passenger planes and crashed them. Thousands of civilians had been killed, and major buildings were damaged.

U.S. troops were seen as a powerful army by some, but to others, the United States was viewed as a bully, one that would send in its army whenever its government didn't agree with that of another country. For example, Iraq was a country with a ruthless dictator that the U.S. opposed. It was not clear whether Iraq was directly involved in the terrorist acts when the United States invaded.

The tsunami gave the United States a chance to change its bully image. Some people criticized its actions, saying they were done only for image, but American troops were sent and tons and tons of aid were delivered.

President George W. Bush pledged $350 million in financial aid, up from the $15 million he had pledged at the onset of the tragedy. He ordered military units to assist whoever asked for help, including Indonesia—the most Muslim country in the world. In fact, the area of Aceh, Indonesia, had been closed to foreigners for many years because Islamic extremism had started to take hold there.

But this was a time to put aside differences and embrace similarities. It was a time to forge new friendships and build trust. Indonesia opened its doors to many countries that sent soldiers. Troops from countries close to Indonesia, like Australia and Singapore, arrived right away, while soldiers from Spain, France, Korea, Japan, and Denmark had to travel a while before getting there.

"We haven't always had the greatest relationship with Indonesia," said Captain Joseph Plenzler, spokesman for U.S. military operations in Indonesia. "But we are here at the request of the Indonesia government. I would say this is a good chance for us to forge a new relationship with them—one built in trust."[8]

Only Indonesian soldiers were allowed to carry guns during rescue and recovery efforts after the tsunami. Military personnel from other countries did not carry weapons.

"It feels strange being in a strange land without my weapon, but we are here on humanitarian efforts," said one U.S. Marine after spending time in Banda Aceh.

Two U.S. Navy ships provide support for tsunami victims in Meulaboh, Indonesia.

The United States was one of the first countries to respond to tsunami-damaged areas with military strength on humanitarian missions. U.S. Navy and Marine vessels responded quickly from bases in the South Pacific including Okinawa.

The World Responds

The Indian Ocean was calm again. It was peaceful, beautiful, the way millions of people knew it before an earthquake caused it to swell and then swallow thousands of people.

The ocean looked as if it had gone back to normal. But the world was different. Somehow it had gotten smaller, and people seemed closer together.

While large relief organizations such as Red Cross International, UNICEF, and World Care were mobilizing and sending teams of doctors and humanitarian workers to the area, schoolchildren around the globe were collecting money. They held car washes or sold lemonade to raise money for victims.

Rock and pop stars were staging fund-raising concerts or simply donating large sums of money from their bank accounts. Prominent people were pressuring well-to-do friends to help. Many of the Internet news sites also collected donations for various charitable organizations. The world was responding.

Not many people from Southeast Asia lived in Brevard County, Florida. Yet when Indian cancer doctor Silas Charles decided to raise money for victims of the tsunami, people came through in a big way. The doctor's goal was to raise $100,000. Between December 26 and January 7, he wound up raising $200,000.

One of his colleagues, a fellow Indian doctor, perhaps summed it up best.

"It's important that we all come together and show that we are humans first, not Muslims or Hindus or whatever," she said. "It is time we all work together and show the Earth that we are all human beings."[1]

Some people criticized the United Nations, the European Union, and the United States for not responding quickly enough. But how could anyone have guessed the severity of this disaster? Nothing like this had ever happened before.

Once the shock wore off, aid began pouring in from all directions.

By sea, two American aircraft carriers, the USS *Abraham Lincoln* and the USS *Bonhomme Richard,* were dispatched from their locations near Japan to the Indonesian coast and near Sri Lanka, very close to where the tsunami destroyed cities. From these stations, they could ferry in one helicopter after another to deliver medicine, food, and water to those in need.

By air, the Australian and Singaporean air forces set up airstrips in Medan, Indonesia. They flew large cargo planes and transported helicopters full of food, water, and medical supplies to hungry survivors at relief sites.

On Friday, January 7, United Nations Secretary-General Kofi Annan flew to the hardest-hit areas. Flying over what had previously been beautiful tourist resorts in Sri Lanka, he was especially moved. Like many in the world, he felt a sadness he had never felt before. "The disaster was so brutal, so quick and so far-reaching that we are still struggling to comprehend it," he said.[2]

But Kofi Annan was also determined to help. With tears in his eyes, he promised food and everyday supplies to every person in need in Sri Lanka. He promised that the world would not forget the people of Asia.

In the United States, American flags flew at half-mast for a week to honor those who perished in the tsunami. President George W. Bush urged Americans to donate money to relief organizations. He named former presidents Bill Clinton and George H. W. Bush to lead fund-raising efforts at home. He vowed that Americans were committed to seeing Asia's massive rebuilding and recovery efforts all the way through.

He also praised the world for how people responded.

"I commend those individuals, countries and international organizations that are donating money, supplies, transport, logistics and personnel to help those in the path of the tsunami," the president said. "Together, people across the globe are providing relief to those countries."[3]

Finally, in northern Sumatra, in Indonesia, where the most people died, soldiers were able to begin the daunting task of clearing the roads so that trucks could pass through. Then patches of land were cleared so that helicopters bearing relief supplies and doctors could land.

The Red Cross set up camps in the countries hit hardest by the tsunami. Doctors and nurses volunteered from all over the world. Soon,

Singapore, one of Indonesia's closest neighbors, sent relief in the form of humanitarian aid, military relief, and medical supplies. On the outskirts of Meulaboh, the Singapore Red Cross set up tents along the main road that served as makeshift hospitals and medical clinics.

The Red Cross set up camps in countries hit by the tsunami.

many groups had converged on the area. Yet many people were still not receiving the help they needed. Why?

Not only were there the expected obstacles of impassable roads, there were guerrilla fighters as well. Ironically, the countries most affected—Indonesia, Sri Lanka, and India—all had rebel activity or secessionist movements where the tsunami hit: Aceh in Indonesia, the eastern shore of Sri Lanka, and Tamil Nadu (TAH-mul NAW-doo) in India.

Secessionists are a segment of the population that is unhappy with the present government. They want to break away and form a separate country. Some relief agencies were hesitant or leery of going into northwest Sumatra because they were afraid of the rebels. There were rumors that the rebels would kidnap Westerners and steal their supplies.

Dr. Jeffrey Hammond is an Australian who has lived in Indonesia for more than twenty years. He so fell in love with the country that he started his own charity, Bless Indonesia Today, or BIT. He was not intimidated by a rebel threat.

Because of his knowledge of the country, he was able to maneuver back roads and get medical teams to disaster sites. He also was able to organize digging teams that would be able to drill new wells for drinking water.

For Hammond and his crew, the task was both daunting and heartbreaking. "Up the road from a village that was no longer there, was a mass grave," Hammond said. "The people were throwing bodies of babies into the grave like they were throwing out bags of trash. There was no dignity in it. I just wept."[4]

Despite the horrors he saw, Hammond continued to supervise medical teams in that region.

For other relief teams in Indonesia, the frustration of not being able to reach certain areas was growing. Using the Novotel Hotel in Medan as their headquarters, military and international relief workers tried coordinating the massive effort from hundreds of miles away. So many people wanted to get to the site and help, but there was only a limited number of helicopters and planes that could get them there.

"We understand your frustration," said a United Nations representative to scores of relief workers from France, Spain, and Mexico. "Once we have provisions for you to go, mainly transportation, then we will prioritize and get the people we need most to the regions where they are needed."[5]

Even those that somehow forced their way into the Aceh province of Indonesia were sometimes stopped by Indonesian soldiers. The soldiers were under strict orders by the government to keep watch over relief workers.

Kiok Chandra, an insurance agent from Jakarta, took a ship to Meulaboh (MOO-la-bow), Sumatra, with about 200 volunteers who were all experienced in disaster relief work. They ran into a roadblock. Soldiers would not let them into the area to help. Chandra and his volunteers waited eight days off the Sumatra coast.

"We are very frustrated," Chandra said as they waited. "We want to help but we are under orders from the army. Everyone is so anxious to work with the foreigners who are coming to help us."[6]

Slowly but surely, relief began to get through and people would soon start trying to live their lives again.

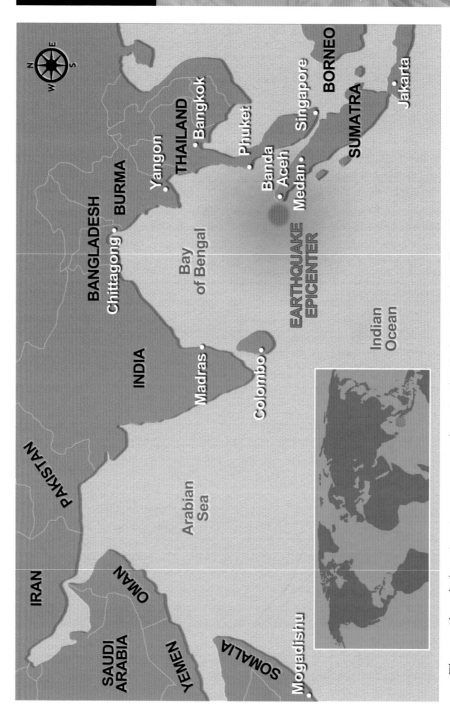

The earthquake's epicenter was very close to the Indonesian shoreline. The ensuing tsunami traveled the length of the Indian Ocean, all the way to Africa.

FOR YOUR INFORMATION

The people in Aceh, Indonesia, where the tsunami killed over 140,000 people, had been shut off from the Western world for many years. The government had not allowed visitors into that area for fear they would get hurt by fundamentalist Islamic rebels wishing to form their own state. When international relief workers were needed to provide humanitarian efforts, the government relaxed its stance and allowed people to go to Aceh.

Even though the government had changed its mind, the question remained: Would it really be safe to travel there? There had been horror stories of people having their limbs hacked off or of being kidnapped or killed.

"Stay on the main roads because there have been shootings and rebel activity," warned Major Andrew Tan of the Singaporean army as relief workers checked into Aceh.[7] He was helping coordinate efforts in Meulaboh.

On the other hand, an Australian military commander just a few hours earlier said things in Aceh were perfectly safe.

"The reports on the television have been overblown," he said from the military headquarters in Medan. "The Indonesian Army is doing a good job at security and keeping everyone feeling safe."[8]

Still, reports of fighting between rebels and government soldiers caused the United Nations to keep its relief workers out of the area for a few days beginning January 17, 2005. While neither the rebels nor the government would confirm the fighting, one thing was clear: It was the people who needed the help that would continue suffering if the fighting continued.

From his jungle hideout, rebel leader Tengku Mucksalmina assured the safety of relief workers. "Our mothers, our wives, our children are victims from this tragedy," he said. "We want them [aid groups] to stay. We ask them not to leave the people who are suffering."[9]

There was hope that the tsunami would create a climate for peace between the Aceh rebels and the Indonesian government. Peace talks were being held in Finland between the opposing parties. During the last weekend in January, the talks soured. It appeared as if the peaceful climate in Aceh had only been temporary.

Indonesian soldiers sit atop their tanks. Government soldiers have been fighting rebels in Aceh for decades.

The big Favo clock in Meulaboh's town square still stands and is frozen at 7:05.

At 7:05, the exact time the tsunami hit, the water rose up and destroyed the city. At first, people could not stop staring at the grim reminder of the disaster. But after a while, the clock lost its novelty as people tried to get their lives back to normal.

CHAPTER 4

Hope and Miracles

No one looked at the giant clock anymore. For a few days following the December 26 tsunami that devoured up to 80 percent, or 32,000, of the people who lived there, the people of Meulaboh stared in amazement at the giant structure. It had stopped ticking at 7:05 in the morning.

That the clock still stood, with ruins of buildings, homes, and businesses at its feet, was amazing in itself. But people could not get over the time of 7:05 that it showed. At first, people could not stop staring.

It was a way of holding on to the past. It was a way of making time stand still. It was a way to remember the moment when loved ones were still alive. The moment before the water decided to rise up out of the ocean.

But now, a few weeks after digging bodies from the mud and putting them into mass graves, people were ready for time to start moving again. No one looked at the stuck clock anymore. Instead, people started clearing rubble from the roads and their yards. They started to seek the help they needed. They started to move out of their feelings of shock. Their eyes began to show a glimmer of hope.

Hope is a good start for a people whose lives are destroyed, but it would take a lot more than just hope to rebuild Meulaboh. It might even take a miracle.

And miracles come in many forms.

Elvin Bidri of Jakarta joined the relief agency ADRA so that he could help ease the suffering in Aceh—a place he had never been to. ADRA stands for "Adventist Development and Relief Agency International."

This relief group, based in the United States, helps mainly Asian and developing countries. "I came to help my fellow countrymen," Bidri said. "We, the people at ADRA, are working hard to get schools and learning going again. I have spent the last few weeks getting the surviving children to register for school. Then we will have to find or build some sort of infrastructure to hold classes in. This is very important for the people. It's a way of getting their lives started again."

Why did Bidri get involved?

"I saw the suffering and I thought I could help," he said, smiling before getting on a helicopter back to Medan. "But I haven't seen my little daughter in three weeks, so I'm going home for a weekend."[1]

Kate Evans, living in Hong Kong, wanted to repay one miracle with another. On December 26, 2004, Evans had been vacationing with her nine-year-old son, George, at a resort in the tiny country of Sri Lanka. She was eating breakfast up on a hill while George played on the beach.

Before she or anyone else at the resort knew it, the tsunami was upon them and a wave had swept her only son away. She screamed and ran down to the beach into the swirling surf. She grabbed a stick and began poking at the water to see if she could feel her son. She continued screaming and crying. She was sure George had been killed. Some of the resort workers saw her and raced down to save her before she got carried away as well. They promised to help her look for George, but they couldn't find the little boy in the water.

A few hours later, after the ocean water had receded, they took her from temple to temple in a van to see if somehow George had been saved by someone else. Once again, they had no luck. Things were looking grim.

Two hours passed by and the workers decided to try one more place, a little villa where they heard some survivors had been taken. They opened the door to the villa, and standing there, waiting, was George. Cooks at the resort had found him in the water and taken him to safety.

Evans called it a miracle.

When she got back to Hong Kong, she decided to repay the miracle and the people of Talpe (tal-PAY), Sri Lanka. She decided to start raising money for vaccinations and for water purification tablets to help keep the children there from getting sick.

"Thanks to their efforts, we were reunited," Evans said. "I was incredibly moved. They had lost their own children but instead they were helping me."[2]

Evans, a friend, and a doctor returned to the area several times after the killer tsunami and delivered vaccinations and other supplies. She called it just her small way of giving back.

A few weeks after the disaster, the people of the region began smiling, began waving at the scores of foreigners who had traveled very far to help them. They began to say thank you.

They were thanking the world because the world did not abandon them. They were thanking the world for ignoring differences and, instead, embracing similarities.

People were helping each other pick through the rubble that used to be their homes to see if there was anything left worth salvaging. They joined neighbors in helping to clear the mud from their vegetable gardens. Muslims and Christians worked side by side to make living just a little bit easier. People stopped asking why this happened and instead began focusing on what would happen next, how to start rebuilding.

By this time, the death tolls were already up over 200,000, and yet something miraculous was happening. Doctors, experts, and scientists had all predicted that hundreds of thousands more would probably die from diseases that would crop up in the tsunami aftermath. Most of the dangers, they said, would come from contaminated drinking water, mosquitoes, and people living in close quarters in shelters.

Some of the main concerns were cholera, malaria, and pneumonia, started by germs that are spread through air and water. Relief workers and even journalists visiting the area were advised by their doctors to take malaria pills, cholera inoculations, and hepatitis shots.

Cholera is a toxic intestinal infection. It can be spread when untreated sewage reaches the food or water supply. Those afflicted can lose up to two gallons of liquid a day. The disease can kill within hours.

"It's not impossible for the disease to appear out of nowhere," Gregory Hartl of the World Health Organization said about cholera.[3]

Another concern, malaria, usually occurs when there are large pools of stagnant, muddy water lying around. Water had pooled and become stagnant in just about every country that experienced the tsunami. Since mosquitoes, which transmit malaria, lay their eggs in stagnant water, it was important for relief workers to ship the strongest antimalaria medication to the hardest-hit areas.

Influenza and pneumonia were another real danger, since influenza germs are highly contagious. Many of the survivors were forced to move into refugee camps, where they had to live in very close quarters with a lot of other people. Children, elderly people, and those with compromised immune systems were most at risk. Relief workers brought in tons of antibiotics to treat people with coughs or colds.

Antibiotics would also be used to treat tetanus. Tetanus is an infection caused when wounds are exposed to muddy water.

By the beginning of February, signs for the biggest miracle of the tsunami were starting to become clear. There had been no major outbreaks of any major diseases, anywhere. Despite camplike living conditions, the contaminated drinking water sources, and all the standing water that bred mosquitoes, somehow or another an even bigger catastrophe had been avoided.

In Indonesia, hundreds of dead bodies had made the region's main drinking supply unusable. Cleaning the drinking water was especially important. Water purifiers use either ozone, ultraviolet light, or bleach to help make contaminated water safe for people to drink. When gigantic water purifying machines were delivered to the region by the Spanish and Australian governments, the odds greatly improved that people would not get sick on a massive scale.

Joe Hurston consoles a victim of the 2004 tsunami

Governments, smaller groups, and individuals brought water purifying units into the disaster zone. For some, such as missionary Joe Hurston from Titusville, Florida, it took a lot of hope, a true miracle, and a leap of faith to be able to deliver them.

Hurston had seen a lot of suffering and a lot of need in his twenty years as a missionary pilot. Once, after a major hurricane, he flew more than forty missions of mercy in one week from Florida to the Bahamas. He had also done disaster relief work in Haiti.

While Hurston delivered bottled water in his tiny six-passenger airplane, he thought there had to be a more efficient way to bring clean water to the people who really needed it. He wasn't interested in one of those gigantic water purification units. He wanted something he could take to the people that would pump them fresh water.

He teamed up with an Arizona inventor to create the Vortex Voyager water purifier. The unit weighs only 21 pounds and can pump 30 gallons of clean water per hour. In fact, it can turn raw sewage into drinking water in just seconds.

Moments after hearing about the Asian tsunami, Hurston decided to take twenty units to Indonesia. But the units hadn't yet been built or paid for, and he didn't have contacts for delivering them.

"It's a real leap of faith," he said on December 28, 2004, "but I'm going. I don't know when and how, but I am going."[4]

On January 8, 2005, Hurston, his wife, adult daughter, and five others he affectionately called water mules were able to cart the finished units to Jakarta, Indonesia. From there, the group took a plane to Medan, Sumatra, a few hundred miles from the hardest-hit areas.

Once in Medan, Hurston had no way of getting the units to Meulaboh or Banda Aceh. Luckily, he was staying at the Novotel Hotel, where his water purifiers caught the eye of American ambassadors and officers with the Singaporean army. They decided the units were desperately needed and put Hurston and his "water mules" on the next morning's helicopter to Meulaboh—a place not known for welcoming Christian missionaries.

Hurston decided to rely on the small string of miracles and his faith. He delivered the units, donating some to doctors and some to relief organizations. He also was able to get out into one of the poorest neighborhoods and pump clean water to groups of smiling children.

"This thing crosses all denominational and religious barriers," he said. "This is a human thing. Who can argue against getting clean water to drink?"[5]

Volunteers place dry ice on corpses in a
Wat Bang Muang, near Takuapa, Thaila

As of January 7, 2005, more than 5,000 people were listed dead in Thailand following the massive tsunami of December 26, 2004. More than 4,000 people were still listed as missing.

What's Next?

Whenever there is any loss of life, it is hard to compare tragedy and loss. But it would also be hard to argue that anyone lost more than Serasma Bidi of Meulaboh during the December 26 tsunami.

Bidi, like so many others from her hometown, was taken by surprise when the surge of water moving at the same speed as a jet airplane tore through her neighborhood, sweeping loved ones away from her permanently. It all happened so fast that even weeks later she had a hard time remembering the details of the wave that snatched four of her children and her husband, sending them to their death.

All she remembers is being ripped from her home by rushing water. It was so cluttered with debris that it did not even seem to be water at all but just moving wood and concrete and sludge. She remembers screaming, and the screaming of others, heard above the roaring power of the Indian Ocean. She remembers looking for her husband and children. She remembers the crying. She remembers the suffering.

But her suffering did not stop there. When the water dropped back to normal levels and the carnage was over, Bidi counted as forty the number of family members she lost.

"I don't know what to do, I don't know what to do," cried Bidi, tears falling from her face like little glass globes and smashing on the floor. She had spent two weeks at a refugee camp in Medan and was waiting with her two surviving sons to board a helicopter back home. "I have lost everything."[1]

Yet, having lost so much, Bidi was going home to try to rebuild. There is something about the human spirit that will not allow it to completely give up. Even though it had been reduced to a pile of rubble, it was still the only home she knew. It was where she belonged, not in some refugee camp. There is something to be said for familiar ground. Her children smiled; at least they had their mother.

Twenty minutes later even Bidi's spirit seemed lifted as she held her left hand out in front of her and read from the Koran, finding comfort in her religious beliefs.

~

Despite the tenacity of the human spirit and the fact that people will one day recover from this tragedy, the truth remains that if there had been a warning system in place, then many if not most of the victims could have been saved.

The sad thing is that Indonesia was supposed to have one already in place. In fact, Japan had promised the Southeast Asian nation $2 million and to help with the technology to devise a tsunami warning system for the Indian Ocean, similar to the one in place in the Pacific Ocean. Somehow, the offer got lost in the shuffle of Indonesia's government, and nobody followed up on it.

Since the killer tsunami, there have been many high-profile meetings among Asian leaders to discuss implementing a tsunami warning system in the Indian Ocean. One meeting was held in Jakarta, Indonesia, and another in Kobe, Japan.

During the last weekend in January 2005, delegates from 57 nations met in Phuket, Thailand, to discuss where to base a center that would collect oceanographic data and monitor the earthquakes and tremors from nations around the Indian Ocean. The center would be able to issue alerts to coastal areas in danger.

Thailand offered to make Bangkok the base for the center, but as has happened many times in the past, Asian countries could not agree. India and Indonesia did not want the center in Thailand. The countries then agreed to perhaps build several smaller regional centers. Whether they are ever built remains to be seen.

Another suggestion that can save lives in the future is simply to have more cooperation between countries. For example, the Pacific Ocean tsunami warning system received warnings from its computers that something may have been happening in the Indian Ocean. By the time the embassies in the endangered countries were warned, the tsunami had already reached land.

Like the mythical bird the phoenix, born from its own fiery ashes, the countries on the rim of the Indian Ocean now have a chance to re-build—and to become even better than before. Ironically, the national symbol for Indonesia is the Garuda, a mythical eagle that is believed to remove obstacles. In some drawings, the Garuda has the face and wings of an eagle but the body of a man. It will be man, and the great human spirit, that will have to move Asia past this tragedy.

There are some who are already working to improve life for the coastal tsunami survivors. For example, one curiosity is that mangrove trees and large coconut trees were not destroyed by the tsunami's rushing waves. In fact, there are many people who survived the sea surge by climbing to the tops of coconut trees. Some experts are already calling for more mangrove forests and coconut trees to be planted near the coasts. Others are calling on governments to hire more environmental experts to help their countries plan for better and safer coastlines.

"This disaster, ironically, also provides an opportunity to rebuild the region according to a more sustainable path," said Emil Salim, the former state minister of the environment for Indonesia.[2]

Indeed, one of the most amazing survival stories stemming from the Asian tsunami deals with an ancient tribe of people living on the remote Andaman and Nicobar Islands off the Indian coast. While the little islands were pummeled by rising ocean water for hours, the tribes experienced very little loss, despite their ancient and primitive ways. The answer? Some say it is because they were so in tune to their environment.

They believe that the tribes' knowledge of the movement of the wind, ocean, and wildlife may have given them ample warning to reach higher ground.

"They can smell the wind. They can gauge the depth of the sea with the sound of their oars. They have a sixth sense which we don't possess," finds Ashish Roy, a local environmentalist. "These tribes live close to nature and are known to heed biological warning signs like changes in the cries of birds and the behavior patterns of land and marine animals."[3]

The animal world also seemed to know something was coming. There were hardly any reports of wild animals—such as elephants, tigers, water buffalo, or orangutans—being killed. They all made it to higher ground and escaped the coming floods.

There weren't too many dead animals found after the tsunami.

Water buffalo have new territory to wallow in muddy terrain after the tsunami's ocean water subsided. There are many new puddles and mud pits for the animals to explore and root through while they graze for food.

While some were ready to move forward and talk of rebuilding, some of the worst-off areas in Banda Aceh were still suffering immeasurably. A United Nations official said on January 31 that there were more than 800,000 people living in that region who needed to be fed. Their livelihood gone and crops and farms destroyed, these people were relying solely on the work of relief organizations.

Some countries were looking into ways to transform areas ravaged by the tsunami into places that could generate more money for the government and the economy.

In Thailand, government officials were talking with developers. They were considering turning the tiny resort island of Phuket into a duty-free port and allow foreign ownership of land.

"Among all this disaster, it would be a blessing if Phuket was able to reinvent itself," said Australian developer Tony James, who lives in Phuket.[4]

It will take many years for those who suffered and lived through the 2004 tsunami to heal. Some may never get through it. The world will never be the same again. And no matter what the cause—whether it was a punishment from an angry god, a freak of nature, or the result of our disconnection from nature and the environment—one thing is clear. When the world suffered a tragedy like no other, the people of the world responded. For a moment, the world became a friendlier place, one where helping other human beings in need became more important than religion or ethnic background or skin color.

"Thank you," said Zuli Nuzuli, the Muslim man who lost his eighteen-year-old daughter, to American relief workers leaving a plane that had just landed in Sumatra. "Thank you for helping us. You are good people. We love you."[5]

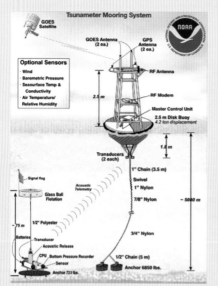

Tsunameter

After the tsunami struck in the Indian Ocean, many people wondered if such a catastrophe could befall the United States. After all, millions of Americans live on U.S. coasts, and tsunamis can be over a hundred miles long.

Tsunamis have struck Hawaii and killed dozens of people. American geologists have been studying and preparing for the possibility of tsunamis hitting the West Coast of the United States, particularly Oregon and Washington State. And some space experts predict that on March 16, 2880, a giant asteroid could fall into the Atlantic, sending a 300-foot-high tsunami up over the East Coast of the United States.[6] The good news, according to scientists, is that there is only a 3-in-1,000 chance of this happening.

Americans are all very lucky to live in a country that has scientific observatories set up that can detect most natural disasters, like tsunamis, well before they happen. There are buoys that monitor the ocean's activity, sensors that sit on the ocean floor, and gauges near the shorelines that measure the height of incoming waves. Chances are if a tsunami were headed for a U.S. coast, there would be enough advance warning to evacuate our families to safety. Of course, if the tsunami were as massive and as lightning-fast as the Indian Ocean tsunami, then chances are people would still die. In the event of a massive tsunami, it would be very difficult to evacuate big coastal cities in time.

Scientists have also predicted that killer tsunamis could strike the nearby Caribbean. The Caribbean Sea, like the Indian Ocean, does not have a tsunami warning system, and the potential for earthquakes is there. In 1946 a tsunami welled up in the Caribbean, but it struck unpopulated areas and did very little damage. Experts say it is only a matter of time before another tsunami hits the Caribbean. Big earthquakes usually happen there about every fifty years, so that area is overdue for one.

The bottom line is that warning systems can save lives, but no one who lives near the ocean is ever entirely safe. Tsunamis, or at least their strength, can be very hard to determine. For example, in 1998 there was a relatively small undersea earthquake off the coast of Papua, New Guinea, that measured 7.1 on the Richter scale. The quake started a landslide under the water that resulted in a surprise tsunami. More than 2,000 people were killed.

Recognizing the warning signs of a tsunami, as ten-year-old Tilly did, can also save lives.

Chronology

November 2004 President George W. Bush is reelected to a second term in the White House

December 25 Christians throughout the world celebrate Christmas

December 26 Shortly before 7:00 A.M., about 100 miles off the coast of Sumatra, a 9.0-magnitude earthquake lifts the ocean floor, starting a tsunami
—Just after 7:00 A.M., the tsunami engulfs Aceh, Indonesia
—About two hours later, it strikes Thailand
—Seven hours after the earthquake, the tsunami reaches the coast of Africa, killing people and damaging property there

December 27 Tsunami death toll is said to be 12,000, but many thousands are still missing

December 28 The United Nations says that the damage caused by the tsunami is unprecedented; the death toll climbs over 55,000

December 29 Tsunami death toll reaches 80,000

December 30 Tsunami death toll reaches 118,000

December 31 The United States pledges $350 million in aid, a large hike after its initial offers

January 3, 2005 The U.S. military begins full-blown relief operations in Southeast Asia; this is the largest American military operation there since the end of the Vietnam War; other countries are also sending troops, including Australia, Singapore, Spain, France, Korea, Japan, and Denmark

January 3 Japan pledges $500 million in aid

January 5 Australia pledges $800 million in aid

January 7 World leaders fly over the affected areas to assess the damage

January 19 Tsunami death toll soars past 212,000; a tsunami warning is issued for Japan after an underwater earthquake is detected, but no tsunami forms

January 29 Talks and hopes for peace break down between the Indonesian government and Aceh rebels

February 10 President Bush asks Congress to increase tsunami aid from $350 million to $950 million

March 28 Hundreds of Indonesians are killed when an 8.7 magnitude earthquake hits Sumatra, only three months after the tsunami devastated the area. A tsunami alert is issued.

April 10 A 6.7 magnitude earthquake takes place in the South Pacific

April 16 Aceh rebels and the Indonesian government report a "breakthrough" at establishing lasting peace

Other Killer Tsunamis

November 1, 1755   More than 60,000 people are killed in Lisbon, Portugal, by an earthquake and the resulting tsunami.

August 27, 1883   After the volcano Krakatau erupts, tsunamis kill about 36,000 people in Indonesian islands of Java and Sumatra.

June 15, 1896   Nearly 27,000 people are killed on the east coast of Japan.

May 22, 1960   Chilean Tsunami hit Japan and Hawaii

August 23, 1976   Close to 8,000 people are killed in southwest Philippines.

October 9, 1995   Manzanillo, Mexico tsunami

July 17, 1998   In Papua New Guinea, three tsunamis kill at least 2,000. Many others injured by the tsunami die of gangrene infections.
—Source: CNN and s2.news.wisc.edu/

For Further Reading

Fredericks, Anthony D. *Tsunami Man: Learning About Killer Waves with Walter Dudley.* Honolulu, HI: University of Hawaii Press, 2002.

Prager, Ellen J. *Furious Earth: The Science and Nature of Earthquakes, Volcanoes, and Tsunamis.* New York: McGraw Hill, 1999.

Sorenson, Margo. *Tsunami! Death Wave.* Des Moines, IA: Perfection Learning, 1997.

Steele, Christy. *Tsunamis.* Orlando, FL: Heinemann Educational, 2003.

Thompson, Luke. *Tsunamis.* Danbury, CT: Children's Press, 2000.

Wade, Mary Dodson. *Tsunami: Monster Waves.* Berkeley Heights, NJ: Enslow Publishers, 2002.

On the Internet
Up-to-date Asian Tsunami Disaster News
http://news.yahoo.com/asiadisaster

News Accounts of Asian Tsunami
http://news.bbc.co.uk/2/hi/in_depth/world/2004/asia_quake_disaster/

Earthquake Hazards Program
http://earthquake.usgs.gov/eginthenews/2004/usslav/

International Tsunami Information Center
http://www.prh.noaa.gov/pr/itic/

Tsunami Database
http://www.ngdc.noaa.gov/seg/hazard/tsu.shtml

Chapter Notes

Chapter 1 The Ocean Moved

1. "Girl, 10, Used Geography Lesson to Save Lives," *London News Telegraph*, January 1, 2005.

2. Personal interview on January 11, 2005 in Medan, Sumatra.

3. Associated Press, "Hero Washed Away Trying to Do One Last Good Deed," *South China Morning Post*, January 10, 2005, p. A9.

Chapter 2 Aftermath

1. Personal interview on January 10, 2005, in Medan, Sumatra.

2. Ibid.

3. Ibid.

4. Kenneth Woodward, "Countless Souls Cry Out to God," *Newsweek*, January 10, 2005, p. 37.

5. Personal interview on January 9, 2005, in Jakarta, Indonesia.

6. French Press Agency, "Survivor's 11 Days Under the Rubble," *South China Morning Post*, January 9, 2005, p. 7.

7. Personal interview on January 9, 2005, in Jakarta, Indonesia.

8. Personal interview on January 10, 2005, in Medan, Indonesia.

Chapter 3 The World Responds

1. Telephone interview on January 5, 2005, in Melbourne, Florida.

2. Associated Press, "Kofi Annan Tours Area," January 8, 2005.

3. "Helping the Tsunami Victims," *The Jakarta Post*, January 11, 2005, p. 6.

4. Personal Interview, January 11, 2005, in Sumatra.

5. Personal observation during an NGO meeting on January 11 at the Novotel Hotel in Medan.

6. Lynne O'Donnell, "Massive Aid Effort Is Not Reaching Those Hardest Hit," *South China Morning Post*, January 10, 2005, p. A8.

7. Personal interview on January 12, 2005, in Meulaboh, Aceh.

8. Personal Interview on January 11, 2005 in Medan, Sumatra.

9. Lely Djuhari, "U.N. Officials Ban Travel in Part of Tsunami-hit Region," Associated Press, January 18, 2005.

Chapter 4 Hope and Miracles

1. Personal interview at a helicopter landing field in Meulaboh, January 13, 2005.

2. Annemarie Evans, "Grateful Mother Comes to Resorts' Rescue," *South China Sunday Morning Post*, January 9, 2005, p. 6.

3. Claudia Kalb, "Waves of Disease," *Newsweek*, January 10, 2005, p. 44.

4. Personal telephone interview on December 28, 2004.

5. Personal interview in a Meulaboh neighborhood on January 13, 2005.

Chapter 5 What's Next?

1. Personal interview at the helicopter landing pad at Polonia Airport in Medan on January 12, 2005.

2. Emil Salim, "Sustainability from Ruin," *The Jakarta Post*, January 11, 2005, p. 6.

3. Global News Wire, "Is the Clock Ticking for the Tribes That Time Forgot?" January 17, 2005.

4. Alan Morison, "Opportunity After Disaster," *South China Morning Post*, January 10, 2005, p. A11.

5. Personal interview on January 10, 2005, in Medan, Indonesia.

6. Jerry Adler and Mary Carmichael, "The Tsunami Threat," *Newsweek*, January 10, 2005, p. 44.

Glossary

cremate (KREE-mayt)
To burn a dead body completely so that only ashes are left.

duty-free (DOO-tee free)
Not requiring taxes to be paid.

Garuda (GAH-roo-dah)
A mythical eagle with magical powers.

guerrilla (GU-ril-a)
A type of warfare that is irregular and is usually waged by units independent of the government.

intimidated (in-tim-e-DAY-ted)
To be frightened by threats.

Koran (KE-ran)
The Muslim book of sacred writings.

mass graves (mass GRAVES)
Large pits in the ground in which large numbers of corpses are buried together.

Richter scale (rik-TER skale)
An open-ended scale that measures the strength of earthquakes; 1.5 is the smallest earthquake that can be felt, and 8.5 or over is very devastating.

tectonic plates (tek-TON-ik playts)
Large pieces of the earth's crust that float on the mantle and on which are continents and oceans. These plates are constantly moving; when they collide, earthquakes result.

tenacity (teh-NAS-ih-tee)
Not giving up or breaking down.

tsunami (SOO-nah-mee)
A large ocean wave caused usually by an earthquake or volcanic eruption.

Author's Note

John A. Torres

I am lucky enough to live across the street from the Atlantic Ocean and a beautiful beach in a place called Indialantic, Florida. While living by the beach has many advantages, in 2004, Florida was hit by four hurricanes. Indialantic suffered three of them, and many homes—including my own—were damaged.

But the damage I saw here in Florida (mainly leaky roofs) was nothing compared to what I saw when I landed in Meulaboh, Indonesia, in January 2005, just weeks after a tsunami there killed hundreds of thousands.

It did not seem real. I felt as if I were walking on a Hollywood movie set. Every house was rubble, every person I spoke to had lost a child or a wife or a husband. I listened to them and I shed tears with them. These people were eager to talk, to share their stories. They were very gracious and very grateful for the world's help. The people of Indonesia touched my heart in a way that I will never forget.

And while I loved being there with them, trying to help them move past this incredible disaster, I also could not wait to get home to my wife and family. We sometimes do not realize how lucky we are. It's easy to complain when we are stuck in traffic or when there are long lines at the supermarket or when there is nothing good to watch on television. But from now on I will try not to complain.

I will try to remember the faces and voices and tears of the people I met in Indonesia. I will try to remember how they have fought and scratched to cling to life without loved ones or houses or jobs or food or water. I will try to remember the hope in their eyes and the smiles on their faces. The next time I am stuck in traffic, I will smile and remember them.

Index